Pebble Plus

Dogs, Dogs, Dogs

All about Beagles

by Erika L. Shores

Consulting Editor: Gail Saunders-Smith, PhD

CAPSTONE PRESS
a capstone imprint

Pebble Plus is published by Capstone Press,
1710 Roe Crest Drive, North Mankato, Minnesota 56003.
www.capstonepub.com

Library of Congress Cataloging-in-Publication Data
Shores, Erika L., 1976–
All about beagles / by Erika L. Shores.
p. cm.—(Pebble plus. Dogs, dogs, dogs)
Includes bibliographical references and index.
Summary: "Full-color photographs and simple text provide a brief introduction to beagles"—Provided by publisher.
ISBN 978-1-4296-8722-5 (library binding)
ISBN 978-1-62065-290-9 (ebook PDF)
1. Beagle (Dog breed)—Juvenile literature. I. Title.
SF429.B3S46 2013
636.753'7—dc23
2011049814

Editorial Credits
Veronica Correia, designer; Marcie Spence, media researcher; Kathy McColley, production specialist

Photo Credits
123RF: Peter Kirillov, 11; Alamy Images: Juniors Bildarchiv, 3, 15; Capstone Studio: Karon Dubke, 1, 19;
Corbis: Karen Kasmauski/Science Faction, 7; iStockphoto: onepony, 13, Pumba1, 9, Sadeugra, 21;
Shutterstock: AnetaPics, 5, 17, Jagodka, cover

Note to Parents and Teachers

The Dogs, Dogs, Dogs series supports national science standards related to life science. This
book describes and illustrates beagles. The images support early readers in understanding
the text. The repetition of words and phrases helps early readers learn new words. This book
also introduces early readers to subject-specific vocabulary words, which are defined in the
Glossary section. Early readers may need assistance to read some words and to use the Table of
Contents, Glossary, Read More, Internet Sites, and Index sections of the book.

Printed in the United States of America in North Mankato, Minnesota.
022013   007184R

Table of Contents

Super-Sniffing Dogs

Beagles are dogs with

a super sense of smell.

They like to sniff everything.

Working beagles put
their noses to the test
at airports. Beagles sniff out
unsafe items in suitcases.

The Beagle Look

Beagles are small to
medium-sized dogs.
They stand 13 to 16 inches
(33 to 41 centimeters) tall
at the shoulders.

Most beagles have coats

that are three colors.

They have tan heads

and black backs.

Their legs are white.

Beagles have soft, floppy ears and big eyes that are brown or hazel. A beagle's ears and eyes give it a sweet, kind look.

Puppy Time

Beagle puppies are curious.

They sniff everything

to find out about their world.

Puppies grow quickly.

Beagles live up to 15 years.

Doggie Duties

Beagles are full of energy.

Owners should make sure

their beagle gets lots

of exercise each day.

Like most dogs, beagles
should be fed twice each day.
Beagles should also go to
a veterinarian for a yearly exam
called a checkup.

Playful Pets

Beagles are playful and loyal.

These friendly dogs are

popular family pets.

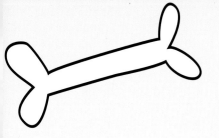

Glossary

coat—an animal's hair or fur

hazel—a light green color

loyal—being true to something or someone

popular—enjoyed or liked by many

sense—a way of knowing about your surroundings

veterinarian—a doctor who treats sick or injured animals; veterinarians also help animals stay healthy

Read More

Beal, Abigail. *I Love My Beagle.* Top Dogs. New York: PowerKids Press, 2011.

Bozzo, Linda. *I Like Beagles!* Discover Dogs with the American Canine Association. Berkeley Heights, N.J.: Enslow Publishers, 2012.

Green, Sara. *Beagles.* Dog Breeds. Minneapolis: Bellwether Media, 2009.

Internet Sites

FactHound offers a safe, fun way to find Internet sites related to this book. All of the sites on FactHound have been researched by our staff.

Here's all you do:

Visit *www.facthound.com*

Type in this code: 9781429687225

Check out projects, games and lots more at
www.capstonekids.com

Index

Word Count: 169
Grade: 1
Early-Intervention Level: 14